1001 Dad Jokes

Totally Terrible Bad Jokes

Printed in the United States of America

First Printing, 2020

ISBN 9781654212612

What happens when a cat wins a
"BEST DOG" contest?
Cat-has-trophy!

What word has five letters but
becomes shorter when you add two
more?
"Short"

I used to hate facial hair.
But then it grew on me.

What does Charles Dickens keep in
his spice rack?
*The best of thymes, the worst of
thymes.*

Dad: My wife is going into labor!
What should I do?
Doctor: Is this her first child?
Dad: No, this is her husband.

What happened when the silkworms
challenged each other to a race?
They ended in a tie.

Job interviewer: In the beginning,
you'll be earning $40,000 and later
that will increase to $60,000.
Dad: Ok, I'll come back later.

Son: Dad I really want to work in
the moisturizer industry, what
should I do?
Dad: The best advice I can give
you is to apply daily.

Boss: How good are you at Power
Point?
Dad: I Excel at it.
Boss: Was that a Microsoft Office
pun?
Dad: Word.

Yesterday, one of my friends told me I often make people uncomfortable by violating their personal spaces.
It was a very hurtful thing to say, and completely ruined our bubble bath.

What creature is smarter than a talking parrot?
A spelling bee.

Why do some people publish long jokes in books?
This isn't where they be long.

How did I get out of Iraq?
Iran!

It takes guts to be an organ donor.

What do you call 52 pieces of bread?
A deck of carbs.

I just spotted an albino Dalmatian.
It was the least I could do to help.

Where do the poor Italians live?
In the spa-ghetto.

With the word 'laughter,' the 'L'
comes first.
The rest of the letters come
aughter it.

What do you call a bunch of crows
inside a tent?
Murder within tent.

Have you visited
www.resetyourvision.com?
It's a site for sore eyes.

I caught my son spray painting
graffiti, and he tried to deny it.
But the writing was already on the
wall.

What would you get if a dinosaur
kicked you in the behind?
A mega-sore-ass.

A lamb, a drum, and a snake fall off
a cliff.
Baa-dum-tsssssssss.

What's Iron Man without his suit?
Stark naked.

You're supposed to put your clock
back in October. But unfortunately,
I can't remember where I got it
from.

I bought some shoes today from a
guy on the corner.
Not sure what he laced them with
but I've been tripping all day.

I hate snakes and worms because
they have no feet. You could say
I'm lacktoes intolerant.

Officer: Do you realize how fast you were driving?
Dad: But you can't give me a ticket, I'm running a marathon today.
Officer: Stop trying to play the race card.

I usually do a pork shoulder when I smoke meat. I thought about changing it up and doing some beef, but I don't wanna brisket.

Dad: Son, you're adopted.
Son: Oh wow I wonder who my real parents are.
Dad: We are your real parents; your adopted parents are the ones picking you up.

I accidentally swallowed a bunch of Scrabble tiles.
My next trip to the bathroom could literally spell disaster.

I'm really upset! Someone stole my limbo stick!
I mean, how low can you go?

I still remember my childhood fondly, when my dad used to roll us down the hill inside of car tires.
Those were the Good Years.

Dad: Judge, fifty percent of my parking tickets are uncalled for!
Judge: Repeat infractions, please.
Dad: Ok, 1/2 of my parking tickets are uncalled for!

I've learned 99% of the English language.
I'm almost their.

My wife has suggested that I register for a donor card.
She's a woman after my own heart.

Have you ever had Jewish coffee?
You'd like it, Israeli good.

My wife tried to unlatch our
daughter's car seat with one hand
and said, "How do one-armed mothers
do it?"
"Single handedly," I replied.

Son: Dad, can you tell me what a
solar eclipse is?
Dad: No sun.

I took my 8-year old daughter to
work yesterday. As we walked
around the office, she started
crying, so I asked her what was
wrong.
My coworkers all leaned in as she
said, "But daddy where are all the
clowns you said you work with?"

Son: Dad, can we have some pets?
Dad: Son, pets are just a step
backwards.

This morning a strange man threw a carton of milk at my car.
How dairy!

What's the difference between a literalist and a kleptomaniac?
One takes things literally; the other takes things, literally.

How do you make a Swiss roll?
You simply push him over.

Justice is a dish best served cold. Because it was served warm it would be justwater.

Gambling addiction hotlines would do so much better if every tenth caller was a winner.

The only thing my friends like doing with me is eating.
I call them my taste buds.

My wife tried to knock me down with an old Elton John record. But I'm still standing.

Why is dark spelled with a 'k' and not a 'c'?
Because you can't 'c' in the dark.

I had a dream the ocean was filled with orange soda.
It was a Fanta Sea.

I used to be addicted to soap.
But now I am clean.

What should you increase to get to the airport faster?
Terminal velocity.

My wife didn't believe me when I said I had made a car out of spaghetti.
You should've seen her face when I drove pasta.

My son begged me to make paper
airplanes with him.
Eventually I folded.

The instructor in my self-defense
class told us the most effective
place to kick a man is his stomach.
Personally, I think it's nuts.

What do you call a man lying in
front of a door.
Mat.

Son: Dad, what is a firefighter's
least favorite letter?
Dad: R, son.

I hate the key E minor.
It gives me the E-B-G-Bs.

What's a goblin's favorite dinner?
Ghoulash.

A farmer who owned 67 sheep asked
me to round them up.
I said, "Sure. 70."

What's Peter Pan's favorite
restaurant?
Wendy's.

How did the Australian let his
brother know that their Dad
called?
"Boomerang, Bro."

When does a regular joke become a
dad joke?
When it's fully groan.

Why is the men's bathroom always on
the left?
Because women are always right.

What should a lawyer always wear
to a court?
A good lawsuit!

I got a promotion at the farm.
I'm the new CIEIO.

I used to make a dad joke every year.
But now I am not sure if I can continue this tradition any father.

My wife was worried about meeting new people on our upcoming cruise.
I said, "Don't worry. We're all in the same boat."

What's the difference between ignorance and apathy?
I don't know and I don't care.

I was asked to help design the first Monopoly game board.
I thought, "I'll give it a go."

I can't find my 'Gone in 60 Seconds' DVD.
It was here a minute ago.

I pushed three drums and a cymbal over a cliff then waited for the punch line.
Ba - dum - bum - CHING!"

I asked my teenage daughter to go get me a newspaper.
She laughed at me and said "Oh, dad, you're so old. Just use my phone."
So I took her phone and slammed it against the wall. That fly didn't stand a chance.

How does Moses make his coffee?
Hebrews it.

What do you call an overused tire?
Tired.

A sweater I bought was picking up static electricity, so I returned it to the store.
They gave me another one free of charge.

My dad used to say, "When one door closes, another opens."
He was a decent philosopher, but a terrible cabinet maker.

Two years ago my doctor told me I was going deaf.
And I haven't heard from him since.

I don't always tell dad jokes But when I do he always laughs!

I saw a man take a gate from my yard. I didn't say anything.
I didn't want him to take a fence.

What happened to the stuttering man who was sent to prison?
He's never going to finish his sentence.

What do you call a musician with no girlfriend?
Homeless.

Which is heavier, a liter of water
or a liter of butane?
The water.
No matter how much you have, butane
will always be a lighter fluid.

I got a really ugly calculator for
my birthday.
But it's what's on the inside that
counts.

A platypus walks into a bar owned
by a duck.
He finishes his drink and asks for
the bill.
So the duck billed platypus.

I've already heard seven cancer
puns today.
If I hear tumor it'll benign.

My uncle died from a turtle
stampede.
It was a very slow death.

As I put my car in reverse, I thought to myself,
"This takes me back."

"Welcome back everybody," is apparently not a good way to start a speech if you're the best man at your friend's second wedding.

What happened to the wooden car with a wooden engine and wooden wheels?
It wooden start.

My father was a conjoined twin so I called his brother my uncle on my father's side.
But when they were surgically separated, he became my uncle once removed.

I once swallowed a dictionary.
It gave me thesaurus throat I've ever had.

My wife said I should try lunges to stay in shape.
That would be a huge step forward for me.

I couldn't understand why my dog was motionless.
Then I realized, it was on paws.

A lion never cheats on his wife.
But a Tiger Wood.

I spent 10 minutes trying to remember what the opposite of "night" was.
In the end, I had to call it a day.

I got fired when I asked a customer if he preferred smoking or non-smoking.
Apparently, the correct terms are "cremation" and "burial".

You can't run through a camp site.
You can only ran, because it's past
tents.

Marriage is like a card game.
At first you have two hearts and a
diamond, but at the end you want a
club and a spade.

What do you call a drunken
dinosaur?
A staggerasauros.

Why was 'E' the only letter in the
alphabet to get a Christmas
present?
*Because the rest of the letters
were not 'E'.*

My wife told me I twist everything
she says to my advantage.
I'll take that as a compliment.

How does Good King Wenceslas like his pizza?
Deep pan, crisp and even.

My wife just accused me of having zero empathy.
I just can't understand why she feels that way.

What did the cannibal choose as his last meal?
Five guys.

I was trying to figure out why the ball kept getting bigger and bigger.
Then it hit me.

Whenever I get into the shower naked, the shower gets turned on.

How much does it cost to park
Santa's sleigh?
Nothing. It's on the house.

Son: I'm cold.
Dad: Go stand in the
corner, it's 90 degrees!

I got into a fight with 1, 3, 5, 7
and 9.
The odds were against me.

The other day I yelled into a
colander and really strained my
voice.

Why do shoemakers go to heaven?
Because they have good soles.

My credit card company must be
really proud of me.
They keep calling me to say I have
an outstanding balance!

What do you call a chickpea that walks off a cliff?
Falafell.

What happens when you eat aluminum foil?
You sheet metal.

My wife bought me a horrible looking leather jacket, but I don't mind wearing it.
I'm easily suede.

My wife is complaining that I'm too impulsive.
How would she know?
We only met yesterday!

Do you struggle to keep your eyes open after using your iPad?
There's a nap for that.

How do you make a waterbed more
bouncy?
Add spring water.

My new dog, Minton, just ate all my
shuttlecocks.
Bad Minton!

Why did the coffee pot file a
police report?
It was mugged.

Why did the invisible man turn
down the job offer?
*He just couldn't see himself doing
it.*

I've started a ship building
business out of my garage.
Sails have literally gone through
the roof!

What do you call a red headed baker?
A gingerbread man.

Dad: Doctor, all four of my boys want to be valets when they grow up.
Doctor: Wow! That's the worst case of parking son's disease I've ever heard of.

What do you call a kid afraid of Santa?
Claustrophobic.

I just got a new job at a prison library.
It has its prose and cons.

People keep asking me to stop naming Bruce Willis movies.
But you know what they say, old habits Die Hard.

When I was in college, my roommate used to clean my room, and I used to clean his.
We were maid for each other.

Have you guys heard the one about the vegan transgender?
He was a her-before.

How do you put a baby astronaut to sleep?
You rocket.

Did you hear about the ATM that got addicted to money?
It suffered from withdrawals.

I asked my wife if I was the only one she'd been with.
She said yes, all the others had been nines and tens.

What do you call a deer with no eyes?
No idea.

Did you hear about the Viking Rudolph the Red? He looked outside one day and proclaimed it was going to rain.
His wife asked, "What makes you say that?"
"Rudolph the Red knows rain, dear."

I don't understand why some people use fractions instead of decimals. It's pointless.

When does a medieval soldier sleep?
Knighttime.

Why were the rappers late for their flight?
They forgot Tupac.

My girlfriend's cell phone service stinks! Eight days ago she said, "We're breaking up." My calls have gone straight to voicemail ever since.

I was attending a noisy trial, and the judge started yelling, "Order! Order!"
So I said, "A pastrami on rye please!"

I arrived early at that new restaurant last night.
"Do you mind waiting for a bit?" The manager asked.
"Not at all" I replied.
"Good, take these drinks to table six," he said.

I told my wife she was drawing her eyebrows on a little too high. She looked surprised.

What do you get when you drop a piano down a mine shaft?
A flat minor.

I broke one of the fingers on my left hand at work today.
On the other hand, everything is alright.

As a hobby my dad stabs watches with a knife.
He says it's a fun way to kill time.

What's the worst thing about ancient history class?
The teachers tend to Babylon.

My friend claims he can build a slingshot with his new 3D printer.
But I'm not impressed; I've had a canon printer for years.

What did the scientist say when he found two isotopes of helium?
HeHe.

I'm going to prison for menslaughter.
Just because I made the men laugh.

Have you heard the news story about the corduroy pillow?
Apparently it's making headlines.

Have you heard about Elton John's new comedy tour?
It's a little bit funny.

What do you say to comfort an English teacher?
They're, there, their.

Sundays are always a little sad.
But the day before is a sadder day.

I found out why nurses carry red
crayons.
In case they have to draw blood.

Is it crazy how saying sentences
backwards creates backwards
sentences saying how crazy it is?

Based upon my shameful behavior
after drinking, I finally decided
to quit drinking altogether.
Now I just drink by myself.

I went to the doctor yesterday and
he says I'm paranoid.
Who else has he told, I wonder?

Marvin Gaye kept sheep in a
vineyard.
He'd herd it through the grapevine.

I saw Arnold Schwarzenegger
eating a chocolate bunny.
I said, "I bet I know what you're
favorite holiday is."
He replied, "Has to love Easter,
baby."

Why do cow milking stools only
have three legs?
Because the cow has the udder.

I asked my North Korean friend how
it was there.
He said he literally couldn't
complain.

What happens when it rains cats
and dogs?
You can step in poodles.

The guy who stole my diary has
died.
My thoughts are with his family.

I called work this morning and whispered, "Sorry boss, I can't come in today. I have a wee cough."
He exclaimed, "You have a wee cough?"
I said, "Really? Thanks boss, see you next week!"

My wife isn't talking to me because apparently I ruined her birthday.
I'm not sure how I did that.
I didn't even know it was her birthday!

Why is German food so terrible?
Because it's the wurst.

I bought a dog from a blacksmith today and as soon as I got home, it made a bolt for the door.

Why do mountains make the best jokes?
Because they're hill areas.

What is the difference between a cat and a comma?
One has claws at the end of its paws, while the other is a pause at the end of a clause.

I showed up at the weekly kleptomaniac anonymous meeting. But all the seats were already taken.

Green is my favorite color. I love it even more than blue and yellow combined.

I stopped at this roadside stand that said lobster tails two dollars. So I paid my two dollars and they guy said,
"Once upon a time there was this lobster..."

How does Frosty the Snowman use the bathroom?
That's snowbody's business!

A Spanish magician told everyone
he would disappear.
He said, "Uno, dos...."
Then disappeared without a tres.

A Russian scientist found the cure
for the common cold.
His name is Medcin Forchestikov.

Ironing boards are just surfboards
that gave up their dreams and got
real jobs.

My friend was upset, so I gave him
ten puns hoping one of them would
make him laugh.
Sadly, no pun in ten did.

The person who invented
autocorrect should burn in hello.

Doctor: Your DNA is backwards.
Dad: And?

Who is bigger, Mr. Bigger or Mr. Bigger's baby?
Mr Bigger's baby, because he's a little Bigger.

What do farmers give their wives on Valentine's Day?
Hogs and kisses.

What do you call a bee that can't make up its mind?
A maybe.

I saw a guy flagging down a taxi van today.
I guess you can say he was Van Halen.

I thought my neighbors were nice people.
Then they went and put a password on their wi-fi.

I visited my friend at his new house. He told me to make myself at home. So I threw him out.
I can't stand visitors.

How many ants does it take to fill an entire apartment building?
Tenants.

What happens if the average number of bullies at a school goes up?
The mean increases.

Mom: Do you think our kids are spoiled?
Dad: No, I think most of them smell that way.

I woke up this morning to find that someone had dumped a load of Lego bricks on my doorstep.
I don't know what to make of it.

My wife is a body builder.
She's pregnant.

What do you call a potato with
glasses?
A spec-tater!

Not to brag but I made six figures
last year.
So they named me the year's worst
employee at the toy factory.

Before I die I am going to eat a
whole bag of unpopped popcorn.
That should make the cremation a
little more interesting.

If you like Christmas so much,
why don't you merry it!

I tried to explain to my four-year-
old son that it's perfectly normal
to accidentally poop your pants.
But he's still making fun of me.

At first I didn't like having a beard.
But then it grew on me.

What's the difference between a dirty old bus stop and a lobster with breast implants?
One is a crusty bus station the other one is a busty crustacean.

I left my wife because she was obsessed with counting.
I wonder what she's up to now?

Dad: I think I have a crush on Beyoncé.
Mom: Whatever floats your boat.
Dad: No, that's buoyancy.

My doctor just told me I'm suffering from paranoia.
Well, he didn't actually say "paranoia", but I could tell that was what he and everyone else were thinking.

Mom: Why are the potatoes burnt?
Dad: That's for tomorrow.
Mom: What?
Dad: It's Black Fry Day.

My wife says I have two faults:
I don't listen and something else.

I saw an ad for burial plots, and
thought to myself this is the last
thing I need.

What kind of fire leaves a room
damp?
A humidifier.

What kind of exercise do lazy
people do?
Diddly squats.

What do ghost pandas eat?
Bam-boo!

Son: The car manual says not to turn up the volume of the stereo maximum.
Dad: Well, that's sound advice.

The only thing Flat Earthers fear is sphere itself.

We all know where the Big Apple is but does anyone know where the Minneapolis?

Statistics say that 1 out of 3 people in a relationship are unfaithful.
I just need to figure out if that's my wife or my girlfriend.

This week's winning lottery numbers are 5, 13, 17, 23, 29, 37 and 41.
I mean, what are the odds?

Chocolate comes from cocoa, which is a tree. That makes it a plant. Therefore, chocolate is salad.

My old English teacher used to fail us for not using the active voice. He was very passive aggressive.

I've just heard that someone stole the 'F' from the Funfair sign in our town.
Now that is just unfair.

I just saw my math teacher lock himself in his office with a piece of graph paper.
I think he must be plotting something.

What do you call a mouse that swears?
A cursor.

I looked longingly into my wife's eyes and whispered, "A...E...I...O...U and sometimes Y."
Best wedding vowels ever.

Why should you never let Eminem vaccinate your newborn?
You only get one shot.

What do you call a musical puppy?
A subwoofer.

What did the boss at the animation studio say when they completed the movie?
"Teamwork makes the Dreamworks."

Juggling seems fun.
But I just don't have the balls to do it.

What is the difference between an African elephant and an Indian elephant?
About 5,000 miles.

I got caught stealing a leg of lamb from the supermarket.
The security guard yelled, "What are you doing with that?"
I replied, "Hopefully going to braise it with potatoes and some gravy would be nice as well."

I spent my day in a well.
It was a day well-spent.

How do people lose their kids in a mall?
Seriously, any tips are welcome.

When my wife went into labor, I was going to tell her dad jokes to try to relax her.
But I was worried about the delivery.

What do you call someone who drills holes?
Boring.

Some mornings I wake up grumpy. On others I let her sleep in.

The average height of a troll is three feet.
That's a little gnome fact.

My favorite word is drool.
It just rolls off the tongue.

Why did the whale cross the ocean?
To get to the other tide.

How many grammar police people does it take to change a light bulb?
Too.

I almost fell down the stairs with a basket of laundry.
I said, "That was a close one." My Dad replied "No, that was a clothes one."

A man came to the doctor with a steering wheel down his pants.
The doctor asked, "What's up?"
The man said, "I don't know but it's driving me nuts!"

I hear they're going to start using herbs to fuel trains.
Maybe ours will now run on thyme.

I kept having nightmares about Cinderella and Peter Pan.
The doctor said I was just having Disney spells.

I hate Russian dolls.
They're so full of themselves.

An Englishman, German, Frenchman and Italian are standing at the side of a street watching a street performer.
The street performer notices they all have poor eye sight so he asks them if they can see him.
They reply, "Yes" "Oui" "Si" "Ja."

England doesn't have a kidney bank, but it does have a Liverpool.

I finally watched Doctor Who. It was about time.

So many people these days are really judgmental.
I can tell just by looking at them.

I hate autocorrect, it always makes me type things I didn't Nintendo!

Every time I get greedy and take more than my fair share, I break out in hives.
I must be allergic to selfish.

My fingers always go numb on the ride into work.
I'm sure it's carpool tunnel syndrome.

Why didn't Dwayne Johnson's downstairs neighbor recognize him?
Because he's been living under a rock.

A Roman walks into a bar, holds up two fingers and says,
"I'll have five beers please."

What did the cat say when it hurt itself?
"Me, ow."

Why was the snowman going through all the carrots?
He was picking his nose!

I've recently developed a severe phobia of elevators.
I'm taking steps to avoid them.

If drug addicts start a relationship, is that considered speed dating or just mething around?

It's sad that Stan Lee died, but at least he lived a Marvel-lous life.

Dogs can't operate MRI machines, but catscan.

What do you call a snowman with a six pack?
An abdominal snowman.

What has 4 letters, sometimes has 9 letters, but never has 5 letters. That's not a question.

What do you call a Mexican bodybuilder who's run out of protein?
No whey Jose.

What kind of doctor is Dr. Pepper?
A fizzician.

What did the farmer say to the cow after night?
It's pasture bed time!

A slice of apple pie is $2.50 in Jamaica and $3.00 in the Bahamas. These are the pie rates of the Caribbean.

How do weak passwords feel?
Insecure.

My secret superpower is detecting Indian flatbread in any given room. My friends all say that's naan-sense.

I am giving up drinking for a month.
Sorry that came out wrong.
I am giving up.
Drinking for a month.

I refused to believe that my road working father was stealing from his job. But when I got home, all the signs were there.

My wife and my kids are leaving me because of my obsession with watching horse racing on TV.
...And they're off!

I hate it when people don't know the difference between "your" and "you're".
There so stupid.

I have been diagnosed with a very specific type of amnesia that causes me to deny the existence of certain 80's bands.
There is no Cure!

A man walks into a seafood store carrying a trout under his arm.
"Do you make fish cakes?" he asked.
"Yes, we do," replied the manager.
"Great," said the man as he points to the fish. "It's his birthday."

A woman and a man were talking when suddenly a bird appeared from the sky.
"Would you like to donate to my charity?" said the bird.
"What is it called?" asked the man.
The bird looked at them and cawed four times.
The man and woman sat very confused until the bird said,
"It's four good caws."

What do you say when you tickle a baby millionaire?
"Gucci Gucci Gucci!"

Why was the pediatrician always losing his temper?
He had little patients.

Just saw a man slumped over his lawnmower, bawling his eyes out. He said he'll be fine; he's just going through a rough patch.

I went to the doctor with a hearing problem.
He said, "Can you describe the symptoms?"
I said, "Well Homer is a bald fat guy and Marge has big blue hair."

When I was a boy, I had a disease that required me to eat dirt three times a day in order to survive. It's a good thing my older brother told me about it.

I think my calendar is trying to kill me.
My days are numbered.

I made some fish tacos last night.
But they just ignored them and swam away.

Why couldn't the bicycle stand up by itself?
Because it was two-tired.

I started my own cooking show in Egypt.
It's called, "Wok Like An Egyptian."

Three weeks ago I sent my hearing aids in for repair.
I've heard nothing since.

How does Santa list the elves on his tax returns?
As dependent clauses.

How do two French men share files electronically?
Pierre to Pierre network.

Two drunk guys were about to get into a fight. One draws a line in the dirt and says, "If you cross this line, I'll smack you in the face."
That was the punch line.

I ordered a giant duck at a fancy restaurant last night.
The bill was huge!

What do you call a hen looking at a lettuce?
Chicken Ceaser Salad.

You have $500. Your daughter texts she needs $200, and your son texts he needs $150.
What do you have left?
Dad: $500 and two unread messages.

How warm was Luke Skywalker in his Tauntaun?
Lukewarm.

What do you call a fake noodle?
An impasta!

My aunt has had the same washing machine since her son Callum died 30 years ago.
I guess washing machines do last longer with Cal gone.

Dad: What does the GPS say?
Wife: You missed a right.
Dad: Thanks babe, you Mrs. Right."

I boiled a funny bone once.
It turned into a laughing stock.

Wife: Stop being an idiot, just be yourself.
Dad: Make up your mind.

How do you think the unthinkable?
With an ithberg!

In a nuclear war, they say the only thing to survive will be cockroaches.
Which means at least we will still have a functioning government.

Went to the doctor and asked him if he had anything for uncontrollable wind.
He gave me a kite.

The scarecrow said, "This job isn't for everyone, but, hay, it's in my jeans."

My wife told me I had to stop acting like a flamingo.
So I had to put my foot down.

What do you call a beat-up Batman?
A Bruised Wayne.

My wife didn't think I'd give our
daughter a silly name.
But I called her Bluff.

What do you call a 60-year-old
whose puberty just started?
A late boomer.

Did you hear about the circumciser
who was fired?
He slipped and got the sack.

There are straight laws...
and there are bylaws.

My wife left me because of my
obsession with astrology.
I guess I should have seen the
signs.

I was in a band during the 80's
called The Prevention.
We were way better than the Cure.

Are glass coffins the latest fashion trend?
Remains to be seen.

What did Yoda say when he first saw himself in 4k resolution?
"HDMI!"

I've just written a song about tortilla. Well, it's more of a rap actually.

What is blue and doesn't weigh much?
Light blue.

The first rule of Passive Aggressive Club is...
you know what?
Never mind.
It's fine.

Where do naughty rainbows go?
Prism.

Why does the sun not need to go to college?
It already has 27 million degrees.

There's a new sport they started at my gym called Silent Tennis.
Apparently it's like regular tennis but without the racquet.

I almost got caught stealing a board game today. But it was a Risk I was willing to take.

I met a vaping vampire from Romania.
He called himself Vlad the Inhaler.

What do you call a beehive with no exits?
Unbelievable.

What did the drummer call his twin daughters?
Anna One, Anna Two.

Wife: I'm not happy with this report card.
Son: Okay.
Wife: I want more A's.
Son: OkAAAAAAAAAy.

Neil Diamond used to be known as Neil Coal until the pressure got to him.

Daughter: What's a light year?
Dad: It's like a regular year but it's lower in calories.

Where does an angry sailor go?
Anchor management.

I know tons of jokes about cash machines.
I just can't think of one ATM.

Believing only 12.5% of the Bible makes you an eighth theist.

Puns leave me numb.
Mathematical puns leave me number.

One time I paid $20 to see Prince
in concert.
But I partied like it was $19.99.

Twenty years ago today I asked my
childhood sweetheart, my best
friend and the most beautiful woman
in the world to marry me.
All three said, "No!"

My wife caught me cross-dressing
and said it was over.
So I packed her clothes and left.

I bet a butcher $20 that he couldn't
reach the meat on the top shelf.
He said, "Sorry man. The steaks are
too high."

What do you call a reluctant potato?
A hesitater.

What is four inches long, two inches wide and drives women crazy?
An empty toilet roll.

Why should you knock before you open the fridge door?
There might be salad dressing.

I was out walking the dogs today and someone asked me if they were Jack Russells.
I replied, "No, they're mine!"

Son: How do you spell "penis"?
Wife: Why?
(pause)
Son: That's it?

I ate my exam paper.
Which means that pretty soon I'll
pass the test.

Not to brag, but I have this
incredible talent of predicting
what's inside a wrapped present.
It's a gift.

Duck walks into a bar.
Duck: "Got any bread?"
Bartender: "No"
Duck: "Got any bread?"
Bartender: "No"
Duck: "Got any bread?"
Bartender: "No, and if you ask me
again I'll nail your beak to this
bar."
Duck: "Got any nails?"
Bartender: "No"
Duck: "Got any bread?"

If pronouncing my b's as v's makes
me sound Russian, then Soviet.

A policeman stops a car.
Policeman: Whose car is this, where are you taking it and what do you do for a living?
Miner: Mine.

When we make pizza at home it's my wife's job to shred the cheese.
She's the gratist!

How much room do fungi need to grow?
As mushroom as possible.

What has four wheels and flies?
A garbage truck.

A pun walks into a bar, ten people die on the spot.
Pun in, ten dead.

What did the left eye say to the right eye?
"Between you and me, something smells."

Someone stole $5,000 worth of Red Bull from a local delivery truck. How do these people sleep at night?

My three favorite things are eating my family and not using commas.

What do you call an alligator with Google Maps?
A navigator.

My son says he hates alphabet soup, though he's never even tried it. Well, he's going to eat his words.

What time does Roger Federer arrive at Wimbledon?
About tennish.

The store near me is having a sale on batteries.
If you buy two packs, they'll throw in a pack of dead ones, free of charge.

Spring is here!
I get so excited I wet my plants!

What do you call a belt with a watch on it?
A waist of time.

Do you know what elves rely on during political campaigns?
Propagandelf.

Went to a nightclub that was full of Orcs, Beasts and Trolls.
It was Mordor on the dance floor.

A man died when a pile of books fell on him. Police said he only had his shelf to blame.

Three men are on a boat. They have four cigarettes, but nothing to light them with.
So they throw a cigarette overboard and the whole boat becomes a cigarette lighter.

What kind of horses go out after dusk?
Nightmares.

Two cats are having a swimming race.
One is called "One two three", and the other "Un deux trois". Which cat won?
"One two three" because "Un deux trios" cat sank.

It's a complete disgrace that gingerbread men are forced to live in houses made of their own flesh.

The final four letters in the word
"queue" aren't silent,
they're just waiting their turn."

What did Jay-z call his wife
before they got married?
Feyoncé.

The guy who invented predictive
text passed away yesterday.
His funfair will be next monkey.

What do you call a man who can't
stand?
Neil.

Mom: Can you make me breakfast in
bed?
Dad: No I'll have to go to the
kitchen.

What's the similarity between playing chess and having a dinner in Australia?
They both end with the checkmate.

How does a vegan begin grace before a meal?
"Lettuce pray."

What did the mouse use to build his house?
Cottage cheese.

I gave my daughter a watch for her birthday. She thought it was so cool and when she showed it to the next-door neighbor. He asked, "That's a pretty watch you've got there! Does it tell you the time?" She laughed, "No, this is an old-fashioned watch. You have to look at it!"

What exactly is an acorn?
Well in a nutshell, it's an oak tree.

What do you call a herd of sheep
tumbling down a hill?
A lambslide.

Do you know what the leading cause
of dry skin is?
Towels.

There are two fish in a tank.
One turns to the other and says,
"Do you know how to drive this
thing?"

I showed the damaged remains of my
luggage to my lawyer, and asked him
if I could sue the airline.
He said I didn't have much of a
case.

What's the fastest liquid in the
world?
*Milk. It's pasteurised before you
see it.*

I was in a restaurant in Paris and ordered the Napoleon Chicken.
When the dish arrived, I was surprised to find it was mostly a carcass.
I asked the waiter why and he said, "We only use the Boneypart."

To the man who stole my weight loss pills,
you have nothing to gain.

What's Beethoven doing in his grave?
De-composing.

What did the pirate say on his 80th birthday?
"Aye matey!"

Friend: Your wife and daughter look like they could be twins.
Dad: Well they were separated at birth.

My wife's leaving me because she thinks I'm obsessed with astronomy. What planet is she on?

I had a Bonnie Tyler GPS but it was terrible.
It just kept telling me to turn around, and every now and then it fell apart.

Who came between Mr. D and Mr. F?
It's a Mr. E!

What did little Johnny's mother do when she caught him zapping the other children with static electricity?
She grounded him.

What's it called when a short man waves at you?
A microwave.

Trying to write some clean jokes about bowling balls, but they keep ending up in the gutter.

My daughter thinks I don't give her enough privacy.
At least that's what she said in her diary.

Which member of ABBA was the oldest?
Bjorn.
It's easy to remember because he was Bjorn before the others.

To the guy who stole my antidepressants,
I hope you're happy now.

Bullets are rather strange.
They only do their jobs after they're fired.

I asked the toy store clerk where the Arnold Schwarzenegger action figures were.
She replied, "Aisle B, back."

What do you call a cheap circumcision?
A rip off.

How does the Pope pay for things on eBay?
He uses his Papal account.

I bought my son a fridge for his birthday.
Can't wait to see his face light up when he opens it.

Honestly, I don't mind leg day at the gym.
It's just the two days after that I can't stand.

Did you know you start out with four kidneys, but lose two of them growing up?
They turn into adult knees.

I just spent $1,000 for a rented limousine and found out it doesn't come with a driver.
Can't believe I spent all that money and have nothing to chauffeur it.

Elon Musk Announces Odd location for New Tesla Factory in the Country of
Mad-at-gas-car.

What do you get if you put a duck in a cement mixer?
Quacks in the pavement.

I can't stand when people kick me in the back of the leg.

What cheese is made backwards?
Edam.

I tried to organize a Hide and Seek tournament, but I eventually gave up.
Good players are hard to find.

For Christmas, I'm getting my kids an alarm clock that swears at them instead of ringing.
They're in for a rude awakening.

I was told that exercise helps with your decision making.
It's true. After going to the gym one time I've decided I'm never going again.

I had a dream where I weighed less than a thousandth of a gram.
I was like "Omg".

If I had to rank you from 1 to 10 on
your ability to pee,
I would say urinate.

Do you guys remember that one hit
wonder by that Gotye guy?
You could say that he was somebody
that we used to know.

What were the lion and witch doing
in the wardrobe?
It's Narnia business.

What nationality is Santa Claus?
North Polish.

People are usually shocked when
they find out I am not a good
electrician.

What sounds like a sneeze and is
made of leather?
A shoe.

Why is it impossible to starve in the desert?
Because of all the sand which is there.

Hansel and Gretel were found in a critical condition. Paramedics have stabilized them, but they're not out of the woods yet.

I went in to a pet shop.
I said, "Can I buy a goldfish?"
The guy said, "Do you want an aquarium?"
I said, "I don't care what star sign it is."

Does refusing to go to the gym count as resistance training?

A guy on a tractor has just drove past me shouting,
"The end of the world is coming!"
I think it was just Farmer Geddon.

Just got back from a job interview where I was asked if I could perform under pressure.
I said I wasn't too sure about that but I do sing a mean Bohemian Rhapsody.

My girlfriend left me saying I am too insecure.
No, wait, she's back! She only went to kitchen.

When I first started dating my wife she asked me what some of my dreams were.
I told her one was about a T-rex who couldn't get a job because his hands were too small and he couldn't tie a tie.
But she meant goals.

You can always distinguish an alligator from a crocodile by paying attention to whether the it sees you later or in a while.

If Snoop Dogg dies before pot becomes legal in all fifty states, he will be rolling in his grave.

My best friend called me and said "An evil wizard turned me into a tiny harp! I don't know what to do!" I went round his house to find out he's a little lyre.

I just saw my friend sweep a girl off her feet.
He's a very aggressive janitor.

Started a new job recently and my wife asked me if there was a gym in my building.
I said, "I'm not sure. I haven't met everyone yet."

I bought a blindfold yesterday. I'm not sure why.
I can't see myself wearing it.

An invisible man married an
invisible woman.
Their kids were nothing to look at
either.

I was walking through a quarry and
said to the foreman,
"That's a big rock!"
"Boulder," he replied.
So I puffed out my chest and
shouted, "Look at that enormous rock
over there, everyone!"

I once asked a taxidermist what he
does for a living.
He said, "Oh, you know...stuff."

I told my wife she should embrace
her mistakes.
And then she gave me a huge hug.

According to some people, the color
of a person's aura changes to cyan
before they die.
Cyan-aura.

I've just burned my Hawaiian pizza.
I should have put it on aloha
temperature.

A lumberjack went in to a magic
forest to cut a tree. Upon arrival,
he started to swing at the tree,
when it shouted,
"Wait! I'm a talking tree!"
The lumberjack grinned and said,
"And you will dialogue."

I just burned 2,000 calories.
That's the last time I leave
brownies in the oven while I nap.

My grandfather's last words before
he kicked the bucket were, "Hey,
how far do you think I can kick
this bucket?"

I remember when plastic surgery
was a taboo subject.
Now when you mention Botox, no one
raises an eyebrow.

Don't be worried about your smart phone or laptop spying on you. Your vacuum cleaner has been gathering dirt from you for years.

I accidentally rubbed ketchup in my eyes.
Now I have Heinzsight.

My boss yelled at me the other day, "You've got to be the worst train driver in history. How many trains did you derail last year?"
I said, "I can't say, it's so hard to keep track."

My wife left me because of my obsession with Linkin Park.
But in the end, it doesn't even matter.

I saw this guy trying to sell something to a cheetah. I thought, "He's trying to pull a fast one."

Son: Dad, whose music did you
listen to when growing up?
Dad: The Clash.
Son: The who?
Dad: Yes, they were good too.

After you die what part of your
body is the last to stop working.
Your pupils. They dilate.

My boss told me to have a good day.
So I went home.

What did the buffalo say to his son
when he left for school?
"Bison."

What do antioxidants and dictators
have in common?
They both eliminate free radicals.

What do you call a funny mosquito?
Malarious!

I insulted my friend Terry in public, and I feel awful.
I must be suffering from dissin' Terry.

Dad: Boss, can I have a week off around Christmastime?
Boss: It's May.
Dad: Sorry. May I have a week off around Christmas?

I hate how funerals are always at 9:00 or 10:00 AM.
I'm really not a mourning person.

What did the grape do when he got stepped on?
He let out a little wine.

What do you call a dog that does magic?
A labracadabrador.

Since getting fired from my job I started a dating site for chickens. I've stopped it though because I was struggling to make hens meet.

I hate conspiracy theories and actually think there's a group of people out there creating them just to annoy me.

What's the difference between a hippo and a zippo?
One's very heavy and the other is a little lighter.

To the man in the wheelchair who stole my camouflage jacket:
You can hide but you can't run.

Dad: Doctor, I think I'm a moth.
Doctor: It's not a doctor you need, it's a psychiatrist.
Dad: Yeah, I was on my way there when I saw your light on!

Bill Nye has a daughter who doesn't believe in science.
Her name is Dee.

What is a dinosaur's least favorite reindeer?
Comet.

I got kicked out of karaoke after singing "Danger Zone" nine times in a row.
Too many Loggins attempts.

My wife told me she thought we'd have less arguments if I wasn't so nitpicky.
I told her, "I think you mean fewer arguments."

"What do you call Santa's most impolite reindeer?
Rudeolph.

How do you make a pirate furious?
Remove the P.

What do you call 2000
mockingbirds?
Two kilomockingbirds.

What did 20 do when he was hungry?
28.

What do you call a man with a
rubber toe?
Roberto.

My wife told me to stop singing "I'm
A Believer" or she'd slap me. I
thought she was kidding.
Then I saw her face.

If I had to rate our solar system,
I'd give it one star.

I was driving to the airport to catch my flight when I saw a sign that said "Airport Left".
So I turned around and went home."

The pulley is the most egotistical of all the simple machines.
It's always the center of a tension.

Today I saw an ad that said "Radio for sale, $1, volume is stuck at max level".
I thought, "I just can't turn that down."

I went to the bar with a boxer but he was only a lightweight.

Why was King Arthur's army too tired to fight?
It had too many sleepless knights.
There's a new Apple service for leaving angry reviews.
iRate.

What's the name of Baby Yoda's mother?
Yomama.

Why did Stalin only write in lowercase?
He was afraid of capitalism.

Wife: You got a vasectomy without telling anyone! Are you kidding me?
Dad: Not anymore.

I am starting a charity to teach short people math.
It's called Making the Little Things Count.

Our maintenance man lost his legs on the job.
Now he's just a handyman.

How does a cowboy start his day?
He reboots.

People often accuse me of stealing other people's jokes and "being a plagiarist".
Their words not mine.

I'm writing a book about basements. I'm hoping it makes the New York Times Best Cellars list.

As a kid I was always made to walk the plank as we couldn't afford a dog.

I was walking past a farm and a sign said "Duck, eggs".
I thought, "That's an unnecessary comma, and then it hit me."

A dad goes into the butchers and says, "Can I have a cut of beef please?"
The butcher says "Lean?"
The dad leans backwards and says, "Can I have a cut of beef please?"

What does Arnold Schwarzenegger say at the beginning of a game of checkers?
"I'll be black."

I told a friend I was off to California this summer.
He told me to be more pacific.
So I went to Hawaii instead.

Did you hear about the mathematician who's afraid of negative numbers?
He'll stop at nothing to avoid them.

God finally answered my prayers for winning the $50 million lottery.
The answer was, "No".

Did you hear about the man who robbed the pastry kitchen?
I heard he was a real whisk taker.

A man is holding a bee, what is in his eye?
Beauty because beauty is in the eye of the bee holder.

Wouldn't it have been amazing if John Lennon had invented that device that you put in your front door to secretly see who's on the other side?
Imagine all the peepholes.

I got mugged by six dwarves last night.
Not happy.

I just swapped our bed for a trampoline.
My wife hit the roof.

My wife said she would stay with me if I promised to stop singing Oasis songs.
I said, "Maybe."

What kind of music does a balloon
listen to?
Pop!

My wife and I have an agreement; I
don't try to run her life, and I
don't try to run mine.

Time flies like an arrow, but fruit
flies like a banana.

Which days are the strongest?
Saturdays and Sundays.
The rest are weekdays.

Why do bees have sticky hair?
Because they use honeycombs.

To the person who stole my coffee,
my lamp and my parrot
I don't know how you sleep at night.

My friends claim I'm the cheapest
guy I know.
Yeah, I'm not buying it.

Why did Tesla read newspapers?
To know about current events.

If I could shoot rockets out of my
feet, I would call them missile
toes.

Some of my friends have been
making very hurtful remarks about
my choosing to wear mittens rather
than gloves.
But I don't like to point fingers.

It's Christmas Day and Mariah Carey
opens her present.
It's a piece of paper saying she's
been given a piece of residential
land but she isn't impressed
stating, "I don't want a lot for
Christmas."

Rick Astley will let you borrow
any movie from his collection of
Pixar films except one.
He's never going to give you Up.

I can't believe that viruses and
bacteria would just invade my body
without a permission.
That makes me sick!

What do you call it when you mix
alcohol and American Literature?
Tequila Mockingbird.

Just broke two of my dad's old
Queen records
Now I want to break three.

I've read so many horrible things
about drinking and smoking
recently that I made a new, firm
New Year's resolution:
No more reading!

I was raised by a pack of wild
hyenas.
Life was tough and food was scarce,
but man did we laugh.

If you've heard of Murphy's Law,
which is anything that can go
wrong will go wrong, then have you
heard of Cole's law?
It's thinly sliced cabbage.

When I was in pirate school I hated
getting my report card.
I always got seven seas.

Why are Irish bankers so
successful?
*Because their capital's always
Dublin.*

Iron Man and the Silver Surfer are
teaming up for the next movie to
fight crime.
They're natural alloys.

I can't believe someone has been underneath my car and stolen my exhaust.
How could anybody stoop so low?

Did you hear about the butcher who fell backwards into his meat grinder?
He got a little behind in his work.

What did one DNA strand say to the other DNA strand?
"Do these genes make my butt look big?"

They really should stock ATMs better. I went to five different ones today and they all said insufficient funds.

What is Beethoven's favorite fruit?
A ba-na-na-naaaaaaa.

My wife said I don't listen to her anymore or something like that.

I was diagnosed as colorblind yesterday. It came completely out of the purple.

I said it once and I'll say it again.
"It."

What do you call a nervous javelin thrower?
Shakespeare.

My wife is pregnant and my doctor asked me if I had ever been present at a childbirth before.
I said. "Yes just once."
He asked, "What was it like?"
I replied, "It was very very dark, then suddenly very bright."

My son is a man trapped in a
woman's body.
He'll be born in August.

Dad: Doc, I can't stop singing "The
Green, Green Grass of Home."
Doctor: That sounds like
Tom Jones Syndrome.
Dad: Is it common?
Doc: Well, it' not unusual.

I was going to start an all cashew
diet, but then I realized that's just
nuts.

My nerdy friend just got a PhD on
the history of palindromes.
Now we call him Dr. Awkward.

What do you call musically-
inclined horse food from the
Netherlands?
Holland Oats.

Why was it called the dark ages?
Because of all the knights.

How did the computer hackers escape?
No idea, they just ransomware.

It's hard to explain puns to kleptomaniacs.
They always take things literally.

People in Dubai don't like the Flintstones.
But people in Abu Dhabi do!

Why can't you breed an eel with an eagle?
It's eeleagle.

I tried calling the tinnitus hotline but there was no answer.
It just kept on ringing.

How do you identify the gender of an ant?
If it sinks, it's a girl ant.
If it floats, it's buoyant.

What do you call it when Batman skips church?
Christian Bale.

I didn't think I was fat until the McDonald's worker said,
"Sorry about your weight."

I took a video of my shoe yesterday.
It was some very good footage.

I'm addicted to ordering hatchets from other countries because of their smell.
I love foreign axe scents.

I have the heart of a lion.
And a lifetime ban from the zoo.

I bought the world's worst
thesaurus yesterday.
Not only is it terrible, it's
terrible.

My dad said I always loved
alphabet soup when I was young.
But it was just him putting words
in my mouth.

What did the volcano say to his
wife?
"I lava you."

I was at the museum and saw a
painting of a bowl, with milk and
some kind of flakes inside.
It was surreal.

I was so angry when the door knob
broke off my front door.
I couldn't handle it.

A man tells his doctor,
"Doc, help me! I'm addicted to
Twitter!"
The doctor replies, "Sorry, I don't
follow you."

I bought an alcoholic ginger beer.
He was pretty happy.

What's a cop's favorite type of
sweater?
A pullover.

I thought I won the argument with
my wife as to how to arrange the
dining room furniture.
But when I got home,
the tables were turned.

What starts with an "O" and ends
with "nions" and sometimes make you
cry?
Opinions.

My wife said, "Don't get upset if
people call you fat.
You're much bigger than that."

My wife told me, "It's over," and
started to walk away.
I just sat there.
I love watching the end credits.

What do you call a bean that's not
cool anymore?
A has-bean.

This website won't let me use
"beefstew" as a password
Apparently it's not stroganoff.

I was struggling to get my wife's
attention.
So I simply sat down and looked
comfortable.
That did the trick.

I named my horse Mayo.
Mayo Neighs.

What do you call a retired miner?
Doug.

What monster likes to dance at a
party?
The boogieman!

People laugh at my car because it's
ugly and green.
But at least I avocado.

What did the nut say when it was
chasing the other nut?
"I'm a cashew."

I'd never sign up to be in a human
cloning experiment. I don't think I
could live with myself.

Why don't people joke about the Jonestown massacre?
The punch line is too long.

It was a bleak day when we heard about the explosion down at the animal shelter.
It was raining cats and dogs!

Radios don't only play music.
That's a stereotype.

A telescope turned up in our yard. We don't know who it belongs to, but we're looking into it.

Someone has been sneaking into my garden and adding top soil.
The plot thickens.

Dad: Doctor, doctor! I keep thinking I'm a woman who delivers babies!'
Doctor: You're just going through a midwife crisis.

A friend of mine has a bank account
only for buying raisins
It's a currant account.

After a long argument with my boss,
I quit my job at the helium factory.
I refused to be spoken to in that
tone of voice.

How does a meteorologist go up a
mountain?
They climate.

My teacher told me I would never
be any good at poetry because of
my dyslexia.
But so far I've made three vases
and a mug.

I'm not sure I believe all this
stuff about genetically modified
food being bad for you.
I had a tasty leg of salmon and I
feel fine.

A dyslexic man walks into a bra.

I've trained my dog to bring me red
wine.
She's a Bordeaux collie.

My wife just told me that Peter
Tork of The Monkees passed away.
I said, "No way!"
Now I'm a bereaver.

I let a pasta chef borrow my car
and he returned it all denty.

What do pigs learn in the army?
Ham to ham combat.

I don't let my kids go online.
There's too many PDF files on there!

What do you call a bulletproof
Irishman?
Rick O'Shea.

Can you believe I was thrown out of my church for claiming Moses spoke with a lisp?
It was a real slap in the faith.

A dog was drowning in a lake and a German man swam out and pulled it to safety.
I asked the man, "Are you a vet?"
The man replied, "Am I vet? I'm soaking!"

I asked my kids if they liked my grandmother.
They said she's a great grandmother.

Instead of a swear jar I have a pessimism jar. Every time I have a negative thought I put a coin in.
It's currently half empty.

What do the French smoke to get high?
Oui'd.

A police officer pulled me over
and said, "Papers."
I yelled, "Scissors!" and drove off.

I bought an Oasis GPS and now all
the roads I have to drive are
winding.

Sometimes I tuck my knees into my
chest and lean forward.
That's just how I roll.

Some people like floors but I'm
more of a ceiling fan.

Have you heard Cyclop's blind
brother?
Neither have eye.

Why was Pavlov's hair so soft?
He conditioned it.

I recently decided to sell my vacuum cleaner. All it was doing was gathering dust.

What did the black pepper say to his wife after coming out of the grinder?
"Don't worry, I'm fine."

What do you call an Egyptian doctor?
A Cairo-practor.

Who is the best at minding their own business?
An entrepreneur.

My wife sighed, "Why does everything have to be a game with you?"
"An excellent question, honey" I said. "But next time, please use the buzzer!"

If good lawyers know the law, what do great lawyers know?
The judge.

My sister majored in philosophy. I saw her sobbing the other day, worried she won't get a job.
I said, "Are you having an existentialist cry sis?"

How do plants get viral infections?
Through the birds and the bees.

I just came home from work when my wife ran towards me and tore off all her clothes.
At that point, my wife flashed before my eyes.

What do you call a cow walking backwards?
Moo walking.

After an unsuccessful harvest, why did the farmer decide to try a career in music?
Because he had a ton of sick beets.

Finally got around to reading that book about clocks!
It's about time!

What do you call your mom's angry French sister?
A Croissaunt.

"You're so childish!" screamed my wife. "Why do you always have to use that stupid walkie talkie with your stupid friends? This is ridiculous, this relationship is over!"
"This relationship is what? Over."

What's an airline pilot's favorite flavor of chips?
Plane.

A man stumbles upon a lamp and a genie pops out and offers him three wishes.
Man: For my first wish I'd like to be rich.
Genie: Alright Rich, what's your second wish?

Why didn't the skeleton want to send any Valentine's Day cards?
His heart wasn't in it.

The man who invented Velcro recently died.
RIP.

I admit I was wrong about how good my chiropractor is.
I stand corrected.

Crocodiles can grow up to 15 feet. But most have only four.

The internet connection at my farm is really sketchy, so I moved the modem to the barn.
Now I have stable WiFi.

I told the doctor I felt like a deck of playing cards.
He said he'd deal with me later.

Of all the inventions in the last 100 years, the dry erase board has to be the most remarkable.

I told my wife that a husband ages like wine. We get better with age.
Then she locked me in the cellar.

My tailor was happy to fix my ripped shirt.
Or sew it seams.

If I ever find the doctor who screwed up my limb replacement surgery, I'll kill him with my bear hands.

Why did the iPhone go to the dentist?
He had a blue tooth.

The first computer dates back to Adam and Eve.
It was an Apple with limited memory, just one byte.
And then everything crashed.

Six thirty is the best time on a clock.
Hands down.

I was on the bus the other day and there was a sign saying, "Do not leave your seat until the vehicle is stationary."
I've been on this thing for three weeks now and it's still a bus.

What do you call a fat jack-o-lantern?
A plumpkin.

My wife warned me that if I took another picture of her, she'd be furious.
That's when I snapped!

My friend asked me if I wanted to hear a really good Batman impression, so I said go ahead.
He shouted, "Not the Kryptonite!"
And I said, "That's Superman."
"Thanks," he replied, "I've been practicing it a lot."

I met a Buddhist monk who refused anesthesia during his root canal surgery.
His aim?
Transcend dental medication.

My wife has this weird OCD where she arranges the dinner plates by the year they were bought.
It's an extremely rare dish order.

Dad: I just heard our child set the school on fire.
Mom: Arson?
Dad: Yes, our son!"

Me and my buddies from work often go to the cheese shop just to shoot the bries.

I asked my wife for an audio book this Christmas, but she got me an encyclopedia instead.
That speaks volumes.

Today I met Bruce Lee's vegetarian brother Broco Lee.

What did the magic fisherman say?
Pick a cod. Any cod.

Yesterday I accidentally swallowed some food coloring. The doctor says I'm OK, but I feel like I've dyed a little inside.

Dad: I can't believe you got me a house for my birthday!
Son: I hope you enjoy it. What are your plans?
Dad: I think I'll just live in the present.

Working at an unemployment office must be so tense.
Even if you get fired you still have to come in the next day.

What's red and smells?
Rudolph's nose.

What do you call a flirty philosopher?
A socra-tease.

What do you call a man who pours a lot of drinks?
Phil.

My grandpa's last wish was that we convert his ashes into a diamond.
That's a lot of pressure.

My wife traumatically ripped the blankets off me last night.
But I will recover.

A vegan said to me, "People who sell meat are disgusting."
I replied, "People who sell fruit and vegetables are grocer."

I told my wife she'd drawn her eyebrows too low.
She just scowled at me.

What did the ghost bring to the party?
Boos.

A man walks into a drug store and says, "Can I have a bar of soap, please?'
The checkout girl says, "Do you want it scented?'
And the man says, "No, I'll take it with me now.'

I always wanted to be a Gregorian Monk, but I never got the chants.

Did you know that diarrhea is hereditary?
It runs in your genes.

There was a big moron and a little moron sitting on a fence. The big moron fell off.
Why?
The little moron was a little more on.

Where do birds meet for coffee?
Nest-cafe.

What's the longest word in the dictionary?
"Smiles", because there's a mile between the two S's.

The local auctioneer has passed away.
He was somewhere around 30,35... 35,40...

I got fired from my lawn maintenance job.
I was just not cutting it.

I asked my date to meet me at the gym and she never showed up.
Guess the two of us aren't going to work out.

Man at grocery store: Are those genetically modified tomatoes?
Store worker: Why do you ask?
Tomatoes: Yeah, why do you ask?

Shout out to people wondering what the opposite of in is.

A duck is standing next to a busy road with cars zooming past while he waits for a break in traffic. A chicken walks up to him and says, "Don't do it, man. You'll never hear the end of it."

A storm blew away 25% of my roof last night
Oof!

I've got a friend who reminds me of a software update.
Every time I see him
I groan, "Not now."

"I got trapped in a bidding war for a house, because my wife loved the lengthy corridor.
Now I'm in it for the long hall.

Why don't ants get sick?
Because they have little anty
bodies.

I would tell you a joke about a
swimming pool, but it's a bit deep.

Even though Spongebob is the main
character, Patrick is the star.

I'd never let my children watch an
orchestra.
There's too much sax and violins.

The recipe said, "Put the stew in at
180 degrees", so I did.
Now it's all over the bottom of the
oven.

What do you call a girl stretched
between two posts?
Annette.

I just found out my mom is the
Tooth Fairy and I'm devastated.
I can't believe she is leaving me
home alone every night.

What do we want?
Low Flying Airplane noises!!!
When do we want them?
Neeeooooooow!

I got my friend an elephant for his
room. He said, "Thanks."
I said don't mention it.

I have a Russian friend who's a
sound engineer.
And a Czech one too, and a Czech
one too.

I once accidentally bumped into
Bono.
He got angry and said,
"Don't push me 'cause I'm close to
the Edge."

I struggle with Roman Numerals
until I get to 159.
Then it just CLIX.

My wife screamed in pain during
labor so I asked, "What's wrong?"
She yelled, "These contractions
are killing me!"
"I am sorry, honey," I replied.
"What *IS* wrong?"

I just found out Canada isn't real.
Turns out it was all mapleleaf.

A termite walks into a bar and
asks, "Is the bar tender here?"

I got sacked from my job as
restaurant manager today after one
of my staff lost three fingers in an
electric food mixer.
Apparently I failed to do a proper
whisk assessment.

A three-legged dog walks into a saloon in the Old West. He slides up to the bar and announces, "I'm looking for the man who shot my paw."

Did you know vampires aren't real? Unless you Count Dracula.

My flat-earther friend decided to walk to the end of the world to prove it is flat.
In the end, he came around.

At the Olympics I saw an athlete carrying a long stick and asked him, "Are you a pole vaulter?"
He replied, "No I'm German, but how do you know my name is Walter?"

Why do bees stay in their hives during winter?
Swarm.

My daughter says she now identifies as a small group of words that have a collective meaning.
Should I be concerned or is it just a phrase?

Every morning at breakfast, I tell my family that I'm going for a jog, and then I don't.
It's my longest running joke of the year.

I just saw a cashier scan the eyes of a rude customer with her barcode reader.
The look on his face was priceless.

For me, the urge to sing "The Lion Sleeps Tonight" is always just a whim away, a whim away, a whim away, a whim away, a whim away...

I tried to cheer my buddy up by inviting him to a poker night after cows broke into his marijuana store and ate all his product.
But he couldn't come, the steaks were too high.

How many bones are in a human hand?
A handful.

At work we have a printer we've nicknamed Bob Marley.
It's always jammin'.

What do you call a dad that has fallen through the ice?
A Popsicle.

If you rearrange the letters of POSTMEN,
They become VERY ANGRY.

I turned suddenly to my son and said, "Name two pronouns!"
He panicked and yelled back, "Who? Me?"

You gotta hand it to short people, because we can't reach it on our own.

Without a doubt, my favorite Robin Williams' movie is Mrs. Fire.

I was drinking my milkshake on a cliff and thought,
"Wow, this is ledge 'n dairy."

Anyone want to buy a broken barometer?
No pressure.

What's the relationship between people buying pizza and people selling it?
They both want each other's dough.

Went to see the doctor about my
blocked ear.
"Which ear is it?" he asked.
"Twenty twenty," I replied.

What do you call a French man
wearing sandals?
Philippe Flop.

What do you call a hen who counts
her eggs?
A mathemachicken.

My twin brother told me he didn't
understand cloning.
I told him, "That makes two of us."

I made a playlist for hiking.
It has music from Peanuts, The
Cranberries, and Eminem.
I call it my Trail Mix.

What is Yoda's last name?
Layheehoo.

I just found out my friend has been living the secret life of a priest.
It's his altar ego.

My friend has designed an invisible airplane.
I can't see it taking off.

"Officer, are you crying while you are writing me a ticket?"
Cop: It's a moving violation.

I asked my friend Sam to sing a song about the iPhone.
And then Samsung.

A warning to the person who stole my glasses: I have contacts!

What do they call a chemist who makes sodas?
A fizzycist.

Why is Thor's friend so relaxed all the time?
I don't know, he's just Loki.

My wife always prefers the stairs, whereas I always like to take the elevator.
I guess we are raised differently.

A cement mixer has collided with a prison van. Motorists are asked to look out for sixteen hardened criminals.

I've been really busy teaching Hobbits how to play cricket.
Bilbo's good at catching, but he can't really Frodo!

My son wanted to know what it's like to be married.
I asked him to leave me alone and when he did I asked him why he was ignoring me.

When is a car not a car?
When it turns into a driveway.

Why is the letter B so cool?
Because it's sitting in the middle of the AC.

Today, I saw someone waving and I wasn't sure whether they were waving at me or at someone behind me.
In other news, I was fired from my lifeguard job.

My buddy said he threw a stick five miles and his dog managed to find it and bring it back.
Seems a bit far-fetched!

My friend couldn't afford his water bill.
So I sent him a "Get well soon" card.

What do you call James Bond in a jacuzzi?
Bubble-O Seven.

A boat builder is showing his son one of his forests. He turns to him and says, "Son, one day this will all be oars."

My wife bought some tickets to go and watch a band called Labyrinth. I don't want to go but it's going to be hard to get out of.

Raw meat used to make me sick. But now I'm cured.

I've just downloaded the Queen movie, Bohemian Rhapsody.
I think it was filmed in a theater though because I see a little silhouetto of a man...

Two windmills are on a date and one asks the other, "So what kind of music do you like?"
The other replies, "I'm a big metal fan!"

As I get older and remember all the people I lost along the way, I think to myself,
"Maybe a career as a tour guide was not the right choice."

I tried drag racing the other day.
It's murder trying to run in heels.

Where did Noah keep his bees?
In his Ark hives.

Dad: My memory is so bad.
Son: How bad is it?
Dad: How bad is what?

A guy is at home when he hears a knock at the door. He opens it and sees a snail on the porch.
He picks up the snail and throws it as far as he can. Three years later there's a knock on the door and he sees the same snail.
The snail says, "What did you do that for?'"

If you cut off your left arm then your right arm will be left.

"What is the difference between unlawful and illegal?
One is against the law, the other is a sick bird.

I couldn't find my car scraper this morning so I had to use a store discount card to scrape the ice.
Didn't really work though,
I only got 20% off.

My best friend's wedding was so beautiful even the cake was in tiers!

Saw a man standing on one leg at an ATM. Confused, I asked him what he was doing.
He said, "Just checking my balance."

A blind person was eating seafood. It didn't help.

For years I was against organ transplants.
Then I had a change of heart.

Two artists had a fight.
It ended in a draw.

What do you call a cow that eats your grass?
A lawn moo-er.

My wife's favorite song is "Ain't No Sunshine" by Bill Withers and she reminds of this every single time it's on the radio.
I reply, "I know, I know, I know, I know, I know..."

I got drunk and drew a graph showing all of the relationships I've ever had.
It had an ex axis and a why axis.

What did the painter do when it got cold?
He put on another coat.

My wife ran off with the guy next door.
I'm really starting to miss him.

I'm trying to be a sociopath, but I'm not that great at manipulating people.
I'm more of a so-so path.

I'm reading a book about WD-40.
It's non-friction.

At first I thought it was great
marrying an archeologist.
But then I found out she was a gold
digger and my life is in ruins.

I was gonna ask which Nirvana
album was the best but then I
thought, "Nevermind."

Yesterday, I gave up my seat on the
bus for a blind person.
Today, I lost my job as a bus
driver.

When a clock is hungry it goes
back 4 seconds.

My wife and I often laugh about how
competitive we are.
But I laugh more.

If I was a superhero I'd be known
as Typo Man.
I write all the wrongs.

What do you call a murderer who
poisons your breakfast?
A cereal killer.

I've just deleted all the German
names from my phone.
Now it's completely Hans-free.

What do you call two worms in
love?
Soilmates.

I bought a really expensive
laxative from the pharmacy.
It gave me a good run for my money.

I heard my son say his first words
to me today,
"Where have you been in the last
20 years?"

If you run in front of a car you get tired; if you run behind a car you get exhausted.

Don't go bacon my heart.
I couldn't if I fried.

My wife said to me that if I got her another stupid gift this Christmas, she would burn it.
So I bought her a candle.

What did the mermaid wear to her math class?
An algae bra.

Where do fish get their money?
The river bank.

My wife asked if she could have some peace and quiet while she tried to cook dinner.
So I took the batteries out of the smoke alarm.

Me and my friends are in a band called "Duvet".
We're a cover band.

What did the French chef give his wife for Valentine's Day?
A hug and a quiche!

I went to the bookstore and asked if they had any books on turtles?
"Hardback?"
"Yes, with little legs."

What do you call a dog with no legs?
You can call him whatever you like, he's never going to come.

Yesterday I saw a guy spill all his Scrabble letters on the road.
So I asked him, "What's the word on the street?"

Did you know that there are no canaries in the Canary Islands?
And the same thing applies to the Virgin Islands.
There are no canaries there either.

Guys, to be frank,
I would have to change my name.

An Iraqi father gave his daughter a large purse for her birthday. She said, "Thanks for the Baghdad!"

What did Luke say to Han and Leia when they split up?
"May divorce be with you."

For the 10th year in a row, my coworkers voted me "The Most Secretive Guy in the Office".
I can't tell you how much this award means to me.

My cross-eyed wife and I just got a divorce.
I found out she was seeing someone on the side.

I love the way the earth rotates.
It really makes my day.

I threw an iPhone into a lake the other day.
It's still syncing.

I was feeling bad about the future today, but then I installed the new version of Office.
It improved my outlook.

Why did 27 eat alone?
Because 28.

I hate spelling errors!
You can mess up just two letters and your entire post becomes urined.

Waiter: How would you like your steak?
Dad: Cooked?
Waiter: Well done?
Dad: Thanks, I'm something of a chef myself.

What lives in the ocean, is grouchy and hates neighbors?
A hermit crab!

Why do cows have hooves?
Because they lactose.

Every morning on my way to work, I slip on the frozen newspaper on our front porch.
I've fallen on some hard Times.

Why did 7 eat 9?
Because you're supposed to eat 3 squared meals a day.

I blame Mother Earth for all
earthquakes.
It's her fault.

I went for an interview at IKEA.
The manager greeted me by saying
"Come in, make a seat."

If the number 666 is considered
evil, then technically 25.8069758
is the root of all evil.

Welcome to the plastic surgery
addiction support group.
I see a lot of new faces.

What do you call friends you like
to eat with?
Tastebuds.

Why should you never throw away
an old dolphin?
*Because they can easily
be re-porpoised!*

A Jamaican man has stormed into my hairdressers and demanded I give him a new style.
I'm dreading it.

People have always told me that "icy" is the easiest word to spell.
And now that I look at it I see why.

I went into an Apple store without showering and everyone started glaring at me.
I said, "What? It's not my fault you don't have windows!"

A photon checks into a hotel.
The bellboy says, "Do you have any luggage sir?"
The photon replies, "No, I'm travelling light."

What do you call 2 guys sitting on top of a window?
Kurt and Rod.

My friend gave birth to a baby boy in the car on the way to the hospital.
Her husband named the kid Carson.

What do you call a bird that drinks too much?
An owlcoholic.

Did you know that Mr. Spock actually had three ears?
A left ear, a right ear and a final front ear.

Dad: What's the difference between an elephant and a matterbaby?
Wife: What's a matterbaby?
Dad: Nothing, but thanks for asking!

If your can opener can't open a particular can, it becomes a cannot opener.

I looked across the museum hall and spotted my ex-girlfriend but I was too self conscious to say hello.
There was just too much history between us.

If anyone wants to come and talk about why my stuff keeps getting stolen the door is always open.

I went into a pet shop and asked for twelve bees. The shopkeeper counted out thirteen and handed them over.
"You've given me one too many," I said.
"That one is a freebie."

My ex-wife hated my obsession with horoscopes. It taurus apart.

A writer approached me today and asked me to help him find his back garden.
I think he lost the plot.

The first day of school, I signed up for English, math, science, and geography.
The rest, as they say, is history.

Waiter: Do you want a box for your leftovers?
Dad: No, but I'll give you an arm wrestle.

I was really mad at my buddy Mark who borrowed my dictionary and refused to return it.
I said; "Mark, my words!"

What type of blood do you give a pessimistic person?
B positive.

A weasel walks into a bar.
The bartender says, "Wow, I've never served a weasel before. What can I get you?"
"Pop," goes the weasel."

What kind of shoes do bakers wear?
Loafers.

I taught my four year old son how to use the word abundance in a sentence.
He said, "Thanks Dad, that really means a lot!"

What do you call a farmer that doesn't like tractors anymore?
An extractor fan.

What did the blanket say as it was falling off the bed?
"Oh sheet!"

They should make another Taken movie, about Liam Neeson being underappreciated for trying to keep his family safe.
Taken 4: Granted

Why were Indiana Jones, Lara Croft, and Nathan Drake depressed?
Their careers were in ruins."

I just had my photo taken with REM.
That's me in the corner.

I was in a taxi today and the driver said, "I love my job. I'm my own boss. Nobody tells me what to do."
Then I said, "Turn left here."

I have a very good feeling about my job interview today.
The manager said they were looking for somebody responsible.
"You've found your man," I said, "whenever there was a problem at my last job, they always said that I was responsible!"

What did the yoga instructor say to his Mom when she tried to leave?
"Nah ma stay."

We're going to have an entire year
of bad puns about vision.
I can see it clearly.

I just lost 20% of my couch.
Ouch.

Why do vampires hoard stocks?
*Because they're terrified of
stakeholders.*

I'm not a competitive person.
I'm always the first to admit it.

What do you do when you see a
space man?
Park your car, man.

Wife: I'm pregnant.
Dad: Hi pregnant, I'm dad.
Wife: No, you're not.

My girlfriend poked me in the eyes so I stopped seeing her for a while.

My boss told me that as a security guard, it's my job to watch the office.
I'm on season 6 but I'm not really sure what it's got to do with security.

Did you know that statistically 6 out of 7 dwarves aren't Happy?

My friend just called me in tears. His wife has left him, taken his Bob Marley collection and his vodka! Poor guy. No woman, no Sky!

True fact: before the crowbar was invented most crows drank at home.

I never make mistakes.
I thought I did once, but I was wrong.

I don't trust stairs.
They're always up to something.

I saw my wife, slightly drunk, yelling at the TV: "Don't go in there! Don't go in the church, you moron!"
She's watching our wedding video again.

Why does Waldo wear a striped shirt?
Because he doesn't want to be spotted.

My wife first agreed to a date after I gave her a bottle of tonic water.
I Schwepped her of her feet.

How do fleas travel from place to place?
Itch-hiking!

Getting my toy drone stuck in a tree isn't my least favorite thing. But it's definitely up there.

My first girlfriend was a tennis player but she broke my heart.
It was like love meant nothing to her.

You'd think a snail would be faster without its shell, but it's actually more sluggish.

I have a contact lens problem.
I have no contact lens solution.

My brother can do motorcycle stunts on the ice.
It's wheelie cool.

A car's weakest part is the nut holding the steering wheel.

I was addicted to the hokey pokey, but I turned myself around.

All my colleagues at work call me "Mr. Compromise".
It's not my first choice of nickname, but I'm ok with it.

My neighbors listen to really good music whether they like it or not.

What do you call a man with a flatfish on his head?
Ray.

I've been told I'm condescending.
That means I talk down to people.

I quit my job as a postman on my first day, right after they handed me my first letter to deliver. I looked at it and said, "This isn't for me."

A moment of silence for our dear friend, liquid water, who did not survive the 100 degree temperature. You will be mist.

What do you call a man who's been dead 10,000 years? *Pete.*

My boss at Pixar and I got into a fight over our lack of new movies. But then we made Up.

Women call me ugly until they find out how much money I make. Then they call me ugly and poor.

My wife is threatening to kick me out of the house because of my obsession with acting like a news anchor.
More on this after the break.

Can February March?
No, but April May.

As soon as space travel is possible, I'm moving from the Milky Way galaxy to the Soymilky Way galaxy. I'm galactose intolerant.

I am addicted to brake fluid.
But I can stop when I want.

Why are old people's feet in such rough shape?
Because time wounds old heels.

I love telling dad jokes.
Sometimes he laughs!

In college I was so broke I couldn't afford the electric bill. Those were the darkest days of my life.

What happened when the red ship crashed into the blue ship?
The crews were marooned.

My wife left me when I became a contortionist.
I should be sad, but I'm knot.

A man in an interrogation room says, "I'm not saying a word without my lawyer present."
"You are the lawyer," says the policeman.
"Exactly, so where's my present?" replies the lawyer."

Before my surgery my anesthetist offered to knock me out with gas or a boat paddle.
It was an ether/oar situation.

What would you say if you had
breakfast with the Pope?
Eggs, Benedict?

What color is the wind?
Blew.

What do you call a chicken looking
at lettuce?
Chicken sees a salad.

A thief broke into my house last
night looking for money.
So I got out of bed to look with
him.

My wife just told me to put the
toilet seat down.
I don't know why I was carrying it
around in the first place.

Can ants erode wood?
No, but a termite.

My neighbor really annoyed me yesterday by playing the same Lionel Richie song over and over again
It was all night long.

My grandfather is 85 and he still doesn't need glasses.
He drinks straight from the bottle.

I once gave my wife the silent treatment for an entire week. At the end of the week she declared, "Hey, we've gotten along really well lately!"

Singing in the shower is all fun and games until you get shampoo in your mouth.
Then it's a soap opera.

What subject does a witch teach at school?
Spelling.

I went to a fancy dress party dressed as an alarm clock but I left early in a bad mood.
The people there kept winding me up all night.

How do you spell candy with two letters?
C and Y.

My daughter asked me what "inexplicable" means.
I said, "It's hard to explain."

The pessimist sees a tunnel. The optimist a light at the end of the tunnel. The realist sees a train. The train engineer sees three idiots on the railroad tracks.

What is a geologist's favorite music genre?
Rock.

My wife said she saw a bowtie made from solid mahogany.
She said she nearly bought it for me but she didn't think I would wear it.
I replied, "Wooden tie?"

The human cannonball tells the circus owner he is going to retire.
"But you can't!" protests the boss.
"Where am I going to find another man of your caliber?"

I used to sell security alarms door to door, and I was really good at it. If no one was at home I would just leave a brochure on the kitchen table.

Who is the greatest chicken killer in Shakespeare?
Macbeth because he did murder most foul!

I asked my chef friend how hard it would be to make a stir fry in a meadow?
He said it was just a wok in the park.

To ride a horse or not to ride a horse.
That is equestrian.

My wife accused me of being immature.
I told her to immediately get out of my fort.

My wife saw me sneezing in the bathroom and said it was gross.
I said, "It's snot!"

"What kind of vitamin improves your eyesight?
Vitamin see.

I've been prescribed
anti-gloating cream.
I can't wait to rub it in!

I used to have a job collecting
leaves. I was raking it in.

"How did the farmer find his
daughter?
Tractor.

I got tired of flipping the little
switch on my rear view mirror to
dim the headlights.
So I removed the mirror and
haven't looked back since.

What do you get when you throw a
hand grenade in a French kitchen?
Linoleum Blownapart.

Sometimes I talk to myself when I'm
alone and it's kind of sad.
"Me too."

I got a rejection letter from the
Origami University today.
I'm not sure what to make of it.

The police just knocked at my house
to tell me my dog was chasing a kid
on a bike.
I just closed the door because my
dog doesn't even have a bike.

"In college, I double-majored in
accounting and dentistry.
Now I can crunch numbers and numb
crunchers.

Why did Waldo wear stripes?
Cause he didn't want to be spotted.

I went to the shop to buy 6 cans
of Sprite.
It's only when I got home I
realized I picked 7-up.

I accidentally ran into a guy that once sold me an antique globe.
It's a small world.

I want to hear 99 people sing "Africa" by Toto.
It's something that a hundred men or more could never do.

I met a nice girl at a bar last night and asked her to call me when she made it home.
She must be homeless.

Apparently Tolkien considered setting The Lord of the Rings in Antarctica until he was told that the place was uninhobbitable.

What does a house wear?
Address.

Why can't humans hear a dog
whistle?
Because dogs can't whistle.

My parents always tell me their
world doesn't revolve around me.
So I guess that means I'm not
actually their sun.

How do you stop a dog from barking
in the back of a car?
Put him in the front.

My dad died last year when my
family couldn't remember his blood
type for the blood transfusion.
As he was dying he kept on
insisting to "be positive", but it's
very hard without him."

Earlier today someone sent me a
bunch of flowers with all the buds
cut off.
I think I'm being stalked.

At my last job interview, I was asked what my greatest weakness was. I said, "Honesty."
The interviewer said, "I don't think honesty is a weakness."
I replied, "I really don't care what you think."

"What do you call a male hacker's clothes?
Malware.

My dad was very upset when our bunnies escaped.
Hare loss is his worst fear.

My girlfriend told me she was leaving me because I keep pretending to be a Transformer.
I said, "No, wait! I can change!"

Elton John hates ordering Chinese food.
Soy seems to be the hardest word.

Which is heavier, the collected works of Shakespeare or a prison full of inmates?
The prose outweighs the cons.

Her: What do you do?
Me: I race cars.
Her: Do you win many races?
Me: No, the cars are much faster.

When I was ten my mom told me to take my brother to a movie so she could set up for his surprise birthday party.
It was then I realized he was her favorite twin, not me.

A construction worker walks into a bar with a slab of asphalt. The bartender asks, "What can I get you?""
The construction worker says, "One beer for me and one for the road."

I used to date a girl with one leg
who worked at a brewery.
She was in charge of the hops.

I went to the zoo and saw a
baguette in a cage.
The zookeeper told me it was
bread in captivity.

I dig
you dig
we dig
they dig
he digs
she digs

It's not a beautiful poem but it's
deep.

My pregnant wife asked me if I was
worried the temperature inside her
would be too hot for the baby.
I said, "Nope. It's womb
temperature."

I recently bought a new toilet brush.
Long story short, I'm going back to paper.

Why do North Koreans draw the straightest lines?
Because they have a supreme ruler.

My son was spending too much time playing computer games, so I said, "Son, when Abe Lincoln was your age, he was studying books by the light of the fireplace.
He considered this for a moment and replied, "When Abe Lincoln was your age he was The President of the United States."

They all laughed when I said I wanted to be a comedian.
Well, they're not laughing now.

What do you call a bee that lives in America?
A USB.

I called my wife and said that I would pick up pizza and coke on the way home from work.
She still regrets letting me name the kids.

I never understood why people dislike vegans so much.
I have never had a beef with them.

Why was Adel's phone bill so high?
Because she must of called a thousand times.

My wife found out I was cheating on her, after she found all the letters I was hiding.
She got so mad and said she's never playing Scrabble with me again.

What do you call a boat full of
polite football players?
A good sportsman ship.

Why don't attractive Spanish people
use umbrellas?
*Because the rain in Spain falls
mainly on the plain.*

What did Tennessee?
The same thing as Arkansas.

I just got back from Dubai where I
was offered 40 camels for my wife.
I usually only smoke Marlboro, but
hey a deal's a deal.

The world champion tongue twister
got arrested the other day.
I heard they're going to give him
a tough sentence.

What did sushi A say to sushi B?
"Wasabi!"

My friend moved to a new house
recently, so I bought him a
housewarming gift--
a radiator.

I've just bought the personalized
license plate BAA BAA.
For my black jeep.

I got fired from my job at the bank
today.
An old lady asked me to check her
balance, so I pushed her over.

What's E.T. Short for?
*So he can fit in his tiny
spaceship.*

Sorry for all the animal jokes, but
alpaca a few more in before I'm
done.

How did the pirate get his ship so cheap?
It was on sail.

What kind of cookwear do Indian restaurants use?
Naan stick pans.

Did you know that a raven has 17 rigid tail feathers called pinions, while a crow only has 16?
The difference between a raven and a crow is just a matter of a pinion.

Atheism is a non-prophet organization.

Chinese deliverty - $20.
Cost of delivery - $4.
Opening the bag to find out they've forgotten part of your order?
Riceless.

Why do all beaches smell of urine?
Because the sea wee'd.

This may be the wine talking,
but I really, really, really,
really love wine.

I saw my wife using her phone to
record herself getting a haircut.
I think she plans to look at the
highlights later.

They've opened a gym where the
instructors go from door to door to
tell people about the benefits of
joining it.
It's called *Jehovah's Fitness*.

I didn't eat anything other than
brown bread for dinner. That was
my wholemeal.

My wife and I had an argument about
which vowel is the most useful.
I won.

My mate set me up on a blind date
and he said, "I'd better warn you,
she's expecting a baby."
I felt like such an idiot sitting
at the bar wearing a bib.

Jokes about unemployed people
aren't funny.
They just don't work.

What did 2 tell 3 when he saw 6
acting like an idiot?
Don't worry about him, he's just a
product of our times.

How many tropical birds does it
take to screw in a lightbulb?
Two-can.

What do you call a tired skeleton?
The Grim Sleeper.

To the guy who stole my antidepressants the other day. I hope you're happy now.

(At a parole hearing.)
Judge: Why should you be released early?
Man: I'm...
Judge: Go on.
Man: I think...
Judge: Yes?
Man: Can I please finish my sentence?
Judge: Sure. Parole denied."

What do you call a bear that's stuck out in the rain?
A drizzly bear.

What's made of brass, and, sounds like Tom Jones?
Trombones.

I can't believe I was arrested for impersonating a politician.
I was just sitting there doing nothing.

Did you hear about the semicolon that broke the law?
He was given two consecutive sentences.

Sadly, I've lost 20% of my sight.
Sigh...

Why don't pirates travel on mountain roads?
Scurvy.

Why did the rapper get gold teeth?
He wanted to put his money where his mouth was.

Give a man a fish and you will feed him for the day.
Teach a man to fish and he's going to spend a fortune on gear he'll only be using twice a year.

Women really know how to hold a grudge over the smallest things. My wife asked me to pass her the lip balm, and by mistake, I gave her a tube of Super Glue.
It's been a week now and she's still not talking to me.

My ex left me because, according to her, I'll never amount to anything.
Fifteen years later, I have one thing to say to her,
"Lucky guess."

Starting your own garden is easy, but picking all of the vegetables? That's the harvest part.

I'm really worried about Jerusalem
being recognized as the new
capital of Israel.
Who's going to Tel Aviv?

Turned 18 today, so I bought a
locket and put my own picture
in it.
Guess I really am independent.

It's our wedding anniversary today.
My wife and I have been happily
married for two years now-
1995 and 2009.

Did you know that 97% of the world
is stupid?
Luckily I'm in the other 5%.

I have been diagnosed with a
chronic fear of giants.
Feefiphobia.

Where do you find giant snails?
On giant's fingers.

The guy who invented the TV remote
control has died.
He's to be buried between two
cushions on a sofa.

What is the most ironic name for a
vegan?
Hunter.

Wife: Just look at that couple down
the road, how lovely they are.
He keeps holding her hand, kissing
her, holding the door for her.
Why can't you do the same?
Me: Are you crazy? I barely know
that woman!

What do you call a sad cup of
coffee?
Depresso.

What do you call a wandering caveman?
A Meanderthal.

I took a pole today and found out that 100% of people get upset when a tent falls on top of them.

When do people start using their trampolines more?
Spring time.

I went to a haunted bed and breakfast in France.
The place was giving me the crepes.

What did the green grape say to the purple grape?
"Breathe out you idiot!"

What type of rock is never delivered on time?
Slate.

What do you call Indiana Jones in a Scandinavian river?
Harrison Fjord.

Why can't Stevie Wonder see his friends?
Because he's married.

I ordered a chicken and an egg from Amazon.
I'll let you know.

So a vowel saves another vowel's life the other vowel says,
"Aye, E! I owe you."

My wife broke up with me recently because I'm a compulsive gambler.
All I can think about is how to win her back.

What's a cannibal's favorite snack?
A knuckle sandwich.

I went to a psychic and knocked on
her front door.
She yelled, "Who is it?"
So I left."

What do you call a psychic midget
who has escaped from prison?
A small medium at large.

If I had a dollar for every time I
didn't know what was going on, I
would be like, why am I always
getting this free money?

I love jokes about the eyes.
The cornea the better.

Why did the Hotel Clerk feel
uncomfortable at work?
It was a hostel work environment.

What is a sausage made up of
annoying children?
Bratwurst.

What do you call a small mother?
A minimum.

Where do beekeepers stay on
vacation?
Air bee and bee.

Wife: This isn't working between us.
For starters, I'm sick of your
stupid jokes.
Me: I see. And for the main course?"